THE
Missionary
Congregation,
Leadership,
& Liminality

Christian Mission and Modern Culture

EDITED BY
ALAN NEELY, H. WAYNE PIPKIN,
AND WILBERT R. SHENK

In the series:

Believing in the Future, by David J. Bosch

Write the Vision, by Wilbert R. Shenk

Truth and Authority in Modernity,
by Lesslie Newbigin

Religion and the Variety of Culture,
by Lamin Sanneh

The Mission of Theology and Theology as Mission,
by J. Andrew Kirk

*The End of Christendom and the Future
of Christianity*, by Douglas John Hall

A Spacious Heart: Essays on Identity and Togetherness,
by Judith M. Gundry-Volf and Miroslav Volf

*The Missionary Congregation, Leadership,
and Liminality*, by Alan J. Roxburgh

THE
Missionary
Congregation,
Leadership,
& Liminality

ALAN J. ROXBURGH

TRINITY PRESS INTERNATIONAL
Harrisburg, Pennsylvania

First published by
TRINITY PRESS INTERNATIONAL
P.O. Box 1321
Harrisburg, PA 17105
U.S.A.

Trinity Press International is part of the Morehouse Group.

Copyright © 1997 Alan J. Roxburgh

Scripture quotations are from the Revised Standard Version Bible, copyright 1973, Division of Christian Education of the National Council of the Churches of Christ in the United States of America, and are used by permission.

Library of Congress Cataloging-in-Publication Data
Roxburgh, Alan J.
    The missionary congregation, leadership, and liminality / by Alan J. Roxburgh.
        p.   cm. – (The Christian mission and modern culture series)
    Includes bibliographical references.
    ISBN 1-56338-190-7 (pbk. : alk. paper)
    1. Missions – Theory. 2. Missions – North America. 3. North America – Religion – 20th century. 4. Christianity and culture – North America – History – 20th century.   I. Title. II. Series: Christian mission and modern culture.
BV2063.R64   1997
266'.001 – dc21   96-49154
                                                            CIP

Printed in the United States of America

        02   03   04   05   7   6   5   4

Contents

Preface to the Series

Both Christian mission and modern culture, widely regarded as antagonists, are in crisis. The emergence of the modern mission movement in the early nineteenth century cannot be understood apart from the rise of technocratic society. Now, at the end of the twentieth century, both modern culture and Christian mission face an uncertain future.

One of the developments integral to modernity was the way the role of religion in culture was redefined. Whereas religion had played an authoritative role in the culture of Christendom, modern culture was highly critical of religion and increasingly secular in its assumptions. A sustained effort was made to banish religion to the backwaters of modern culture.

The decade of the 1980s witnessed further momentous developments on the geopolitical front with the collapse of communism. In the aftermath of the breakup of the system of power blocs that dominated international relations for a generation, it is clear that religion has survived even if its institutionalization has undergone deep change and its future forms are unclear. Secularism continues to oppose religion, while technology has emerged as a major source of power and authority in modern culture. Both confront Christian faith with fundamental questions.

The purpose of this series is to probe these developments from a variety of angles with a view to helping the church understand its missional responsibility to a culture in crisis. One important resource is the church's experience of two centuries of cross-cultural mission that has reshaped the church into a global Christian *ecumene*. The focus of our inquiry will be the church in modern culture. The series (1) examines modern/postmodern culture from a missional point of view; (2) develops the theological agenda that the church in modern culture must address in order to recover its own integrity; and (3) tests fresh conceptualizations of the nature and mission of the church as it engages modern culture. In other words, these volumes are intended to be a forum where conventional assumptions can be challenged and alternative formulations explored.

This series is a project authorized by the Institute of Mennonite Studies, research agency of the Associated Mennonite Biblical Seminary, and supported by a generous grant from the Pew Charitable Trusts.

Editorial Committee

ALAN NEELY
H. WAYNE PIPKIN
WILBERT R. SHENK

Introduction

The central and urgent question for Christian mission in North America focuses on the churches and their identity in the culture of modernity. Congregations in this context are in crisis. It is a crisis, not just of internal identity and structures, but one that involves the massive changes that have transformed modernity, shifting the church from the center of culture to perceived margins. As a result of these processes, questions about the nature of a missionary encounter with our culture have reemerged.[1]

Such discussions are not merely academic debates, nor are they of only passing concern to the churches. They require our utmost attention if, as North American Christians, we are faithfully to indwell the gospel in a culture that has disembedded itself from that tradition. One thing is clear; in contrast with the long history of the Christian church in the Western world, congregations must now learn how to live the gospel as a distinct people who are no longer at the cultural center. The emerging experience of the churches is indeed that of being on the culture's margins.

Although this experience of marginality is only now

fully entering the perceptions of congregations and their leaders, it accounts for much of the malaise currently affecting the churches and their leadership. Unless these leaders recognize and understand the extent to which they and their congregations have been marginalized in modernity, they will not meaningfully shape the directions of congregational life for a missionary engagement. The following pages explore this concept of marginality. The primary question is, How does the church in North America most appropriately understand its current situation?

At this point, one of the significant images shaping this understanding is that of marginality. This notion of marginality needs to be investigated. There is, undoubtedly, a large element of truth in characterizing the churches as being in a marginal locale. A shift in place has occurred, and marginality is the language used to describe the church's changed position in relation to modern culture. The churches have lost their social location at the center of the culture.[2] Rather than being viewed as loss, this changed social location may hold the seeds for a renewed witness to the presence of God's kingdom in the world (Lindbeck 1971). What are required at this point in the dialogue about a missionary encounter are not so much solutions and strategies for engagement, as models that enable the churches to locate better their social reality on the new cultural map of North America.

Almost twenty-five years ago, George Lindbeck mused about the sectarian future of the church in North

America. He offered a sociological, not theological, account of the churches and their location in the culture. Lindbeck foresaw a deinstitutionalized future where the churches had been shifted from the mainstream to the margins of culture. For Lindbeck, there was a de-Christianized future ahead in which the church would be sharply distinguished from the society at large. The future would be "a world in which the majority of people were indifferent or hostile, for either secular or religious reasons, to anything which could claim to be distinctively Christian" (:229). That future has now arrived. In North America, the Canadian experience of marginality and secularization is more advanced than in the United States. The future for the churches is seen more evidentially in the Canadian setting where decline and marginalization have progressed at a more alarming rate. In the United States, this remains a more gradually emerging reality.

Marginalization is the new language used to describe the experience of the church in modernity. For George Hunsberger (1991), it is experienced as a crisis and loss of social function by churches. He suggests that this changed social location can be described in two parts: first, the caretaker days of the churches are over; and second, modern culture — in which the churches find themselves — is itself undergoing fundamental transformation. The first element in Hunsberger's analysis refers to the much-discussed end of Christendom. This means the churches can no longer assume that they are the priests and pastors of the culture. The second element is a much larger issue of modernity's own transformations within which the churches are in a position quite different from that of the margins. Both of these facts have created a crisis of identity for the churches and raised once again the question of a missionary engagement with our culture.

Marginalization has become a defining reality for churches. It is important to explore what this means and how it might be viewed in a constructive way. The transitions facing the churches are vast, requiring their radical re-formation into the next millennia. The critical question is, What does this mean for a missionary encounter with our culture? A first step in providing an answer is to understand the situation. The language of marginalization, by itself, may not be the most helpful way either of describing the current setting or of shaping a missionary encounter, but it is language that needs to be addressed.

This question of missionary encounter is approached from three perspectives. The first chapter reviews the discussion of marginalization in relation to the churches and their self-understanding of that context. The second chapter examines Victor Turner's work on liminality, relating it to the church's experience of marginalization. Turner studied marginalization in groups experiencing rites-of-passage rituals in preindustrial societies. The concept of liminality offers a meaningful framework for understanding the church's relationship within modernity. The third chapter outlines characteristics of leadership for missionary congregations.

1

Marginalization, Modernity, and Loss of Center

───────────

Marginality is a word used by an increasing number of Christian thinkers within North America. Other terms are also used to express the same idea. For example, Canadian theologian Douglas John Hall (1993:472), in the words of Albert van den Heuvel, speaks of the *humiliation* of the church. In stark language he refers to the *disestablishment* of the church.

> The extremity within which the disciple community in North America finds itself today is not only the end of an age, it is also the end of a long and deeply entrenched form of the church. The single most far-reaching *ecclesiastical* factor conditioning theological reflection in our time is the effective disestablishment of the Christian religion in the Western world by secular, political, and alternative religious forces (Hall 1989:200–201).

Hall uses the word "effective" to account for the fact that Christians are only now awakening to this disestablishment. This point is illustrated by the reemergence of conversation around the question of a missionary encounter with Western culture itself. We are now coming to terms, not so much with a new reality, as with an awareness of that reality.

The notion of marginalization assumes a certain set of presuppositions and relationships. First, Christianity once held the center ground in Western culture. This was clearly the case at the level of political, social, and economic life. This Christendom church, obviously, no longer exists. Christianity has, in this sense, been marginalized. It no longer holds such a center. Second, marginalization assumes that there remains a center and a periphery in late modernity. From that center all else is defined. Groups within the culture can, therefore, be identified as central or marginal depending on their relationship to the center. Both of these perspectives require investigation. The first is, unquestionably, an accurate assessment; the second requires further elaboration.

The Christendom Argument and the Experience of Marginality

The Christendom argument is an example of this first assumption. The modern era, over a period of several centuries, displaced its parent, relegating Christianity to the public margins in a privatized religion. This was, among other things, a cultural marginalization whereby Christianity was reduced to the private sphere. In this transition, the churches absorbed modernity's individu-

alizing ideologies and reshaped their forms to accommo-
date their new social location. This first form of marginalization has been addressed in many books and essays.
It is currently a major focus of conversation (Hauerwas
and Willimon 1990). As pointed out above, Lesslie Newbigin has helped to clarify the issues around this kind
of marginalization and frame the consciousness for a
new missionary ecclesiology in the West. For over three
hundred years Christianity has been progressively shifted
from its place of public prominence at the center of
Western culture to an increasingly privatized location.
This has gradually come to be interpreted as Christian
life at the edges of the culture. Behind much of the
marginalization language is awareness of a "Christendom" history that shaped the Western churches until
after the First World War. It was based on the deeply
held conviction that the church was moving toward a
triumphant future throughout the world. This Constantinian view was strongly linked to nineteenth-century
optimism and belief in progress. The church was spear-
heading the sweep of a Christian culture across the globe.
As wrongheaded and destructive as these perceptions
may have been, they undergirded the conviction that the
church held a central place in culture. This Constantinian perspective is now effectively dead. And just as
the adoption of the church into the cultural center in
the fourth-century radically changed the nature of its existence, the recognition of its end has created a radical
sense of loss and marginalization to which the churches
are responding in a variety of ways. The fourth and

twentieth centuries form bookends marking transition points in the history of the church. Just as the fourth century adoption of Christianity by Constantine forced the church to struggle with its self-understanding as the new center of the culture, twentieth-century Christians must now struggle to understand the meaning of their social location in a decentered world. Just as the Constantinian settlement forced the church of antiquity to ask itself what it was in relation to Roman society, the church in modernity is being compelled to ask itself that question again.

This marginalization has taken a specific form. Initially, it was a separation from the public sphere. A specific kind of theology had controlled and shaped the social, political, and economic life in Christendom. The church held a public center. In modernity it was shifted to a new and different center. What occurred was the effective displacement of both God and Christian thought as the center of unity and meaning for the culture. Colin Gunton has expressed this change as follows:

> Modernity is the era which has displaced God as the focus for the unity and meaning of being. . . . [T]he functions attributed to God have not been abolished, but shifted — relocated, as they say today. . . . God was no longer needed to account for the coherence and meaning of the world, so that the seat of rationality and meaning became not the world, but human reason and will, which thus *displace* God or the world. When the unifying will of

God becomes redundant, or is rejected for a variety of moral, rational and scientific reasons, the focus of the unity of things becomes the rational mind (Gunton 1993:28).

The autonomous, rational mind assumed the new public center, while God and Christianity were displaced to a new private center. At the heart of the matter lay a rebellion against the oppressive controls of the Christendom culture. In the displacement of this culture was a search for freedom and autonomy from external, heteronomous groundings. Modernity began as a move to untether human life from any external control. This would eventually result in a postmodern description of reality as ungrounded. In the privatization of Christianity was the desire to guarantee freedom for the rational individual. In a culture that remained deeply rooted in a Christendom way of life, this resulted in a gradual switch of religious life into the private realm. This was not the only bifurcation that shaped modernity. As Newbigin has aptly pointed out, a new notion of "fact" appeared. Fact became separated from value, science from ethics, objectivity from aesthetics. Not only a shift of centers took place. This was accompanied by a growing fragmentation that, in late modernity, resulted in the loss of any genuine center that might give the culture coherence.

Christianity was shifted to a private, individualistic center. If some, in the last century, sensed this marginalization as a massive problem for the church, most settled into the new accommodation. But the forces engendered by modernity meant that, at an even more fundamental level, changes were occurring that would mean that Christianity's new social location could be only a stopping point in a larger passage. The forces of fragmentation were shaping a different social reality from that of center and periphery. In the meantime, the churches accommodated themselves to their new situation by adopting and accelerating the creation of this private center (J. Turner 1985). They became the moral chaplains of culture, holding a religious monopoly over the private religious experience of the individual. This accommodation reached its zenith shortly after World War II and found its most expressive form in the emergence of the suburban congregation (Winter 1961). The latter came to represent the majority situation for most mainline and evangelical churches of the predominant white middle class. Although this long-term shift from the public to the private was not without a great deal of struggle and debate, the churches inhabited this social context and flourished within its realm.

Modernity, Loss of Center, and the Experience of Marginality

The second form of marginalization is the most problematic to the churches. North American Christians, no matter where they may live, have awakened to the breakdown of Christendom and the flood tide of pluralism. It is, in fact, no longer our world (Hauerwas and Willimon 1990:17). This awakening occurred at the end of the first long process of marginalization. But the end of Christendom is not the primary shape of change pressing upon the churches. Something else is occurring that accelerates the experience of being a minority group in a new situation. This must be the case, because the public-private detente with modernity was not only well accepted by the churches but was the context in which they flourished with their near monopoly on religious values.

Modernity, in shaping a new set of relationships for society, was not able to create the stable, cultural reality it displaced. This was no simple exchange of centers. The outworking of modernity's own inner logic makes notions of center and periphery irrelevant. Late modernity is a decentered world. This did not happen immediately. The long-established moral, political, and religious centers of the West were carried over into the emerging modernity, though radically transformed in content and relationship. But all the while, the notion of a stable social center within a culture was dissolving; it was becoming less and less an accurate metaphor for what was occurring. The church's monopoly over the private center of religious life could not last because the center-margin structure of society was disappearing.

Center-periphery notions presuppose the stable characteristics of premodern cultures that are not sustained within associational cultures. Modernity has gradually transformed Western societies from the large, folk-type cultures of the late Medieval period into the highly complex, associational societies of late modernity. In the latter, there is no longer center or periphery; no one is on the margins. Put in the language of postmodernity, there are no longer any grand theories of the whole; meta-narratives have been uncovered as collections of context, value-bound positions. There is no longer a consensus about meaning and purpose, values and directions. Without this there can be no center. This is not just a matter of there being no "sacred canopy." What is absent is any sacred or secular center. We are faced with a plurality of values and ends competing with each other in a free market of beliefs. This is the new situation. It is one that requires that the term *marginalization* be used with care.

A Decentered Context for North American Churches

The church's lived experience is marginalization. Marginality, as an experience shaping the life of North American churches, has the power to keep them linked to a center-periphery paradigm. This perspective creates the need either to recover a center or define a new marginal existence. Neither option is helpful. Each represents a misreading of the actual situation in late modernity. The situation must be seen from another perspective in order to respond with new forms of mission in this culture.

The church's minority experience is not, therefore, that of periphery to center but a more generalized, pervasive embeddedness in a complexity and fragmentation that renders center-margin language obsolete. While the state continues to provide a framework for the social life of the culture, the flow of meaning takes place through a vast market of choices. This is the marginalization now experienced by the churches. There is no longer tacit agreement between the public and private worlds where the churches functioned as chaplains to the culture. That was part of the older detente with modernity. In late modernity, the churches increasingly find themselves in a vast free market of spirituality and choices of complex proportions. They have become but one more special interest group anxiously seeking a market niche in the culture.[3]

Complex cultures[4] are characterized by a multiplicity of perspectives and competing voices. In this context of flux and accelerated change, there are many voices claiming a place. Collectively they create a confusing, relativizing sense of choice. The verities of the early modern detente are no longer possible. New rules are being written, and everything seems to be in flux. This is the loss of any meta-narrative, the suspension of belief toward universalizing claims, and a resistant skepticism toward claims of absolute truth. Culture is now an organized diversity with little sense of defining center. If a center-periphery relationship does exist, it is between the urban and nonurban elements of the globalized world. Cities shape the cultural and social realities of people's lives. Ideologies and belief systems exist in a world of heterogeneity and openness to a wide variety of systems of meaning. Cities are, by nature, open to the outside. They constantly create new networks of interconnectedness that combine and recombine belief systems into ever-changing forms. The character of the city is to create openness to all kinds of differing perspectives. "What is involved, anyhow, is an interplay between perspectives.... [T]here are also perspectives toward perspectives, and in the cultural swirl of the city the manifestations of other perspectives are not at a distant horizon, or beyond it, they are reasonably close at hand" (Hannerz 1992:211).

Rather than marginality being the major challenge to the churches, this complex flux of interconnected perspectives is competing for a place in the new center — the urban world. This center has no margins, only the potential swirl of varying forms in an open market of values and perspectives. Quoting from the work of Clifford Geertz, Hannerz uses the analogy of the octopus to capture this new situation:

> The images of a coherence reaching toward perfection are not particularly apt here: the Bach fugue and so forth. Cultures change in ways which some regret and which please others — sometimes, in ways which seem to be to nobody's liking. There are misunderstandings ... and productive confusions. ... But in his storehouse of metaphors for cultural integratedness, Clifford Geertz also has that of culture as an octopus, not the best of coordinated living things (:167).

Our kind of culture bears strong resemblance to this inelegant animal.

> Geertz prefaces his comments on the octopoid character of cultures with the point that systems can

hardly afford to be both very complex and highly interconnected; the combination could immobilize them (:407). Better spurious and alive, then, than genuine and dead (:167f).

North American churches are now only a part, an element, of the inelegant octopus — one of its many legs. They are neither on the periphery nor on the margins, but are definitely in a new social location. For a church that has long assumed its monopoly over the private religious world of modernity's citizens, it does feel like living on the margins. What images will best help the people of God both to understand and to move through this unsettling passage? What kind of identity might the faith community have in this situation? The marginal consciousness of the churches has offered a number of solutions to these questions. Most have been problematic because they fail to understand this decentered shape of late-modern North America.

Aspects of a Marginal Consciousness in Current Pastoral Roles

These are particularly confusing and tenuous days for pastors and congregations. In Canada, attendance decline is pervasive and shows no sign of ending. Membership roles dwindle and churches are graying. These national trends affect all sociological categories (Bibby 1993:3–11). The experience of marginalization in Canadian churches is more advanced than in the United

States. In one medium-sized Canadian city (100,000) no more than 4 percent of the population attend church on a given Sunday. Congregations blame the malaise on pastors. In turn, pastors feel vulnerable, defensive, and confused. Increasing numbers of congregations are firing their leaders. Denominational executives function like firemen, running from one crisis to another. In all of this, little understanding emerges concerning the massive transitions through which the culture is moving. The shared experience is that of loss and marginality. Pastors struggle to understand the changes that have swept over their roles. For many, ministry roles have changed so dramatically that they are simply trying to hold on and survive. The precariousness of these realities makes it difficult for pastors to discuss questions of missionary encounter models.

One way of viewing the marginal experience of the churches is by looking at some of the assumptions guiding pastoral function today. The symbol "pastor" serves as a generic container for the functions of ordained, recognized leadership in the church. Certain overriding images shape this role in modernity. What is important to emphasize is that the context in which pastoral leadership has been shaped is that of modernity. Harvie Conn (1984:263–89) identifies several models on which theological education have been based when he critiques the images of pedagogue and professional as central images of pastoral function in modernity. As pedagogue, the pastor is primarily a teacher, unfolding the concepts in God's Word to the faithful. This role is based on the cultural assumption of a church in the center of a society where people come from their public lives for spiritual instruction. As a professional, the pastor assumes a central functioning role of modernity — the person trained to a level of expertise that, by definition, no other group in the society has. The pastor functions as a high-level acolyte of modernity, owning the expertise necessary to dispense religious care and functions. Congregations become consumers of these professional services. Seminaries are classified as professional schools, like those of law, business, and medicine. Thus the business of the seminary, especially on university campuses, is to train professionals. The seminary has assumed a social function within the canons of modernity. Despite a half-century of discussion about the lay apostolate, clericalization remains entrenched in the churches.

It is precisely these roles that have ceased to be meaningful for the North American church. In complex, associational societies the rituals and symbols of meaning have shifted dramatically. The symbols of pedagogue and professional belong to a period when the pastor did function at the cultural center. But symbols have shifted. In the language of Durkheim, in modern society ritual functions have contracted. Much of Christian ritual and symbol has been shifted from the public realm where they functioned as effective shapers of meaning for a large part of the population. This Christendom role has been replaced by a decentered church catering to individual, personal choice. The shift in symbols has been from normativity to a minority form among a multitude of minorities. Along with this, the symbols of place and identity have also migrated from the religious to more secularized domains. For example, the symbolic power of the pastor or priest as professional and pedagogue in society has shifted to doctor and psychologist. All this contributes to the consciousness of marginality.

This marginalized consciousness of pastors is seen, in the latter half of this century, in the continual search for ways to reconfigure pastoral identity. Attempts at reconfiguration are observed in three current images of leadership. Each represents an essential element of modernity and an attempt to reconfigure pastoral identity in terms of a perceived cultural center. These images show how the marginalized consciousness seeks roads back to an assumed center. Each symbol represents an attempt to overcome the experience of marginality by accommodating to cultural norms. Beneath these images lies anxiety over loss of identity and a searching around for ways to relegitimize identity and place. The three images are the therapeutic, the technical-rational, and the creation of community.

The Triumph of the Therapeutic[5]

The shift of faith to a private center in early modernity, followed by the subsequent fragmentation of that center in late modernity, has resulted in a search for the replacement of a lost faith. That has been found in the therapeutic. In close pursuit of this transposition, pastoral leadership has come to be defined in terms of therapeutic care. To the struggling symbols of pedagogue and professional has been added that of counselor. Pastors became clinicians; they are viewed as part of the so-called helping professions. Soul care is self-discovery with a loss of larger horizon. A paradigmatic model of this accommodation can be seen in programs like Clinical Pastoral Education (CPE). The church attempts to reconnect itself to a center by redefining its basic symbols in terms of that center. Rieff offers the following summary:

> All attempts at connecting the doctrines of psychotherapy with the old faiths are patently misconceived. At its most innocuous, these psychotherapeutic religiosities represent a failure of nerve by both psychotherapists and clergymen. Finally, the professionally religious custodians of the old moral demands are no longer authoritative; although they still use the languages of faith, that mode of moral communication has lost its ties with either the controls or remissions valid among its adherents. . . . It is in this sense that the Christian and Jewish professionals have lost their spiritual preceptorships (1987:257).

The symbolic essence of the church shifted into the center of the prevailing culture. The assumption of therapeutic roles is the anxious search for reintegration. The underlying belief is that the once-held cultural center can be regained by adopting its modalities. The marginalized consciousness of the churches is at work.

Technical Rationality as Pastoral Education

Max Weber focused on the increased processes of rationalization that religion provides for a culture. A characteristic of modernity is the pervasiveness of rationalization through bureaucratic, organizational, and technical structures. In modernity, technical rationality and instrumental reason become prime modes of social function. Calculation and technique are arbiters of purpose and effectiveness. Anxiety over loss of place and decline in the churches translates into a focus on technique and calculation. Emphasis on models of church growth, church marketing, and entrepreneurial leadership reflect the uneasy, marginal consciousness of the churches. Numerical growth is the talisman that all is well with our ecclesiological souls. Guiding pastoral strategy are the cultural values of instrumental rationality, expressed in "if it works and is successful then it is true." Technique is the primary method for reestablishing the church's place in the culture. God is but a legitimating footnote of ecclesiology.

Pastors' workshops are filled with eager acolytes of success receiving their initiation, from Yuppified gurus, into up-to-date techniques for how to ... (fill in the blanks). Business, pop psychology, and psychographics become paradigms for identity and success. The Harvard School of Business, Faith Popcorn, and George Barna are the contemporary saints, revealing how much we mirror the heart of modernity in our leadership.

Pastors reflect upon their settings from primarily a

practical perspective. This is not simply because they must function with the daily exigencies of pastoral ministry in a mundane world, but because they are part of the worldview of technical rationality. The emphasis and popularity of the practical comes at the expense of *theological* reflection. As Ray Anderson (1993:34) points out, the manuals to which most pastors refer in seeking direction for their daily direction are not drawn from Scripture or the texts studied in seminary, but the latest business and psycho-social workbooks.

too true!

The Private World as the Realm of Pastoral Leadership

also outside of scripture

Borrowing language from de Tocqueville, congregations have become enclosed within their own hearts. Pastors lead congregations that have little sense of a vocation as a people called to lives larger than themselves. Preaching, reflecting this cultural captivity, calls parishioners to discover a Jesus who is guarantor of inner personal happiness in a hazardous and dark world. The perilous fragmentation in the larger culture is kept at bay by creating a group of one's own kind, baptized with the same community.

In each of these three responses pastoral leadership is expressed in terms of the immanent values of modernity: personal need, technique, and privatized community. Charles Taylor (1991:1–12) identifies these as primary characteristics of modernity. It is germane to our conversation to compare Taylor's characteristics with the primary themes of pastoral ministry today.

Themes Shaping Modernity	*Themes Shaping Pastoral Ministry*
1. Individualism	1. Care giving/Counseling
2. Instrumental rationality	2. Technique
3. Fragmentation into groups of self-interest	3. Community/Body life

In each case the functional paradigm of leadership is modernity. The marginalized consciousness of the churches has resulted in a variety of movements seeking to reintegrate the church into a perceived cultural center, even though in late modernity this no longer describes the actual social location of the churches. What is required is a model that enables the churches to see their current situation and reflect appropriately on how they may reconfigure their life for mission in late modernity.

2

Liminality: A Model for Engagement

The Meaning of Liminality

Questions of marginality are not for those who have long experienced Christian life as a minority situation in North America, but rather for those who have assumed that their Christian existence is the cultural norm. For the latter, this reality is accounted as a marginalized Christian existence. A helpful framework for interpreting this experience is Victor Turner's notion of liminality. Turner (1969 and 1977), building on the work of Arnold van Gennep, developed the idea of liminality through a study of rites of passage processes in folk cultures. These accounts of liminality offer a way of understanding the church's current experience of marginalization. Liminality is a term that describes the transition process accompanying a change of state or social position. A group moves through what is described as a "tunnel" experience when it is shifted into a marginal situation within the culture (Turner 1974:232). Liminality offers a rich resource of experiential maps that can suggest a way ahead for churches in framing a response to their changed social location.

Originally, liminality was applied to rites of passage processes in preindustrial cultures. Rites of passage are rituals, usually religious in nature, through which individuals are detached from their established and normal role in society by being placed outside the social nexus in an in-between state; and after some ritualized passage of time, they are returned, inwardly transformed and outwardly changed, to a new place and status. Individuals become structurally, and often physically, invisible in terms of the culture's standard definitions and classifications. They lose their identity. Turner gives a specific definition of the term *structure*. His discussion of the term is important. Basing his comments on the work of Robert Merton, Turner does not define social structure in the language of Levi-Strauss as the entities that exist independent of our consciousness of them, even though they govern our existence. For Turner, social structure is "the patterned arrangements of role-sets, status-sets, and status-sequences *consciously* recognized and regularly operative in a given society" (:237). Therefore, liminality is the conscious awareness that as a group (or individual) one's status-, role-, and sequence-sets in a society have been radically changed to the point where the group has now become largely invisible to the larger society in terms of these previously held sets.

Even in this basic definition, it is possible to observe affinities with the current Christian experience of marginality. For the churches, some form of detachment has taken place. This is the primary way in which much of the contemporary writing about the church tends to account for its current sense of being on the margins. But the notion of status- and role-sets becoming invisible has an interesting application to Christian life in contemporary North America. Although this is a more-or-less common experience, certainly in the Canadian setting this kind of invisibility is well advanced. The removal, for example, of Christian symbolism from the Christmas season is a jarring case in point. Some provincial jurisdictions have sought quietly to instruct their civil servants to keep all forms of Christian symbolism from the workplace. Schools are no longer allowed to sing carols in their assemblies. On a national radio program of the Canadian Broadcasting System, the topic of conversation was whether or not it was appropriate to "keep Christ in Christmas." At one level this is equivalent to asking whether it is appropriate to keep baseballs in baseball. The very definition requires their presence. When one reflects on the absurdity of such a question, it becomes clear the extent to which so much has changed for the church. The once visible Christian symbols of Christmas have been rendered invisible. Naturally, Christians in this context feel themselves marginalized. This represents a genuine betwixt-and-between stage for Christians in our culture. At the same time, there appears to be little conversation among leaders of the churches about the kinds of transformation required for an engagement with the culture. In current discussions of the church and its relationship to our culture, the description and diagnosis of this new marginal experience is usually well developed. What is largely absent, however, is an extended discussion of constructive directions for the church. This should come as no surprise. Turner consistently points out that when a group moves into a liminal state, there is an initial period of confusion, a groping about in order to understand the new location. Furthermore, in this early stage, when the group recognizes that it has been separated from its former embeddedness in social roles, this creates the sense of "outsiderhood" (:233). The basic drive of a group in this initial period is to find a way of returning to its former state. The need to put things back together is strong. Again, this describes well the current response of the churches. There has been an awakening to the disturbing new experience of the liminal. The new clothes still feel ill-fitting and out of place. It is as if the once central place of the church has suddenly been removed, and Christians find themselves in a dark tunnel that offers little direction toward the future. All of this is bound to create a desire for returning and recapturing the secure places of the past. What can be observed are strong impulses to strip off this new dress and return to the comfort of the former uniform. But it is in the nature of liminality that no such return to the previous social location is possible. However, for the moment, the impulse and reflex of the churches is in finding a way of return to the cultural center. Clearly, there will need to be some form of re-engagement, but this will not be to the same place nor to any center. On the contrary, if the current liminal ex-

it was the accommodation of modernity that led to marginalization

perience of the church is properly understood, it will be seen as an opportunity to move away from an accommodation with modernity that has been detrimental to the church and its mission. The present liminality is one that offers the potential for a fresh missionary engagement in a radically changing social context. We will return to this point following discussion of the basic notions of liminality.

The Stages of Liminal Transition

But this model is not anything like modern or current culture!

Turner describes three phases of transition in any rites of passage process: *separation, liminal, reaggregation.* His analysis is related to folk cultures that are characterized by highly cohesive social relationships with clearly identified structures and roles within groups. In these preindustrial cultures, rites of passage are institutionalized in the social structures. Consequently, the rites are both a managed and comprehended part of the culture. They are experienced and make sense within a larger framework of meaning. The three phases of separation, liminal (margin), and reaggregation describe how a group is transformed in its outward relationships to other groups and institutions, and, equally important, in its own inner life.

Each of the three stages has specific ritual processes through which the initiate proceeds. In the separation phase the subjects going through the rite of passage are detached from their established, embedded roles. The initiates have had a socially determined and shaped role that has been essential to their sense of place and purpose. These factors have shaped life. Now they are removed, and a fundamental change in social location occurs. This would happen, for example, during puberty. The young boy is separated from the primary matriarchal social nexus of his childhood. This has been his normative place in the society. It represents his self-understanding. This is what it means to be a boy. Suddenly, he is removed from this world and sent out from the larger group into the wilderness, or some other ritual location, to discover the essence of manhood.

As this change occurs, the initiate moves into the second, liminal, phase. This is the place of marginalization or, to use the language of current discussion regarding the church, disestablishment. It is the liminal phase that is of primary interest for the present discussion. In the liminal stage, the group, or individual, is now outside the normative roles and relationships that characterized and gave meaning to their identity. The pubescent boys are sent out from the society to a ritually significant locale to engage in a process of transformation. One is reminded, as an example of the liminal, of the way God dealt with Israel as recorded in the Book of Hosea. God speaks of removing Israel from her normative place as a nation between Egypt and Assyria. God will then take Israel out into the wilderness in order to purify her so that she will become a new bride for the Lord (Hosea 2:14).

The third, and final, phase in the rites of passage is

reintegration into the social group as a new person with a fresh identity. The formerly pubescent boy is returned as a man with a whole new social role among the males of the community. God promises Israel that through the process of wilderness cleansing she will become a new people. This kind of reintegration is possible only after the liminal has been accepted as a marginal experience that leads to a new, transformative relationship with the social structures of the culture. In preindustrial cultures the society remains stable as the initiate is transformed into something new. Reintegration is back into a stable normativity. This is not the case for the church in modern, complex cultures.

With this brief overview of the three stages, it is now necessary to examine in more detail the middle, or liminal, phase. In this stage there are two critical elements: first, the negation of almost everything that has been considered normative, and second, the potential for transformation and new configurations of identity. Because of the latter, the Latin term liminal is used to describe this as a *threshold* experience. This is the potential that lies beneath the church's current sense of marginalization.

The experience of the margins causes a group to feel very vulnerable. In preindustrial societies such vulnerability and anxiety are controlled and shaped by the ritual process that both initiates and accompanies the liminal. The society frames the liminal experience in ritual traditions that compensate for and channel the anxiety and ambiguity. This is what is missing in modern cultures.

Without an overarching framework, that larger reference of meaning is lost. Consequently, vulnerability and
anxiety become the primary, unmediated experience of
groups. As a result, the tendency is to understand liminality in terms of negation, not potential. Liminality is
perceived as a bad thing, an ending, something that needs
to be resisted and reversed. The potential of a new, trans-
forming relationship with the culture does not surface in
the self-understanding of the group.

Because in preindustrial societies liminal rites of passage are normal, they are expected events that give meaning through ritualization. Although containing elements
of crisis, the liminal is a normal event in the scheme of
things. It would process a significant transition on the
calender of a particular society as the liminal is integrated into an overall social process. It makes sense in
the scheme of social transition; the initiate knows that on
the other side there will be a reintegration into the social
nexus. Others have gone ahead; there are models of what
may be expected. This embeddedness in the social system provides meaning in relation to the broader context.
Even though liminality remains a threshold experience,
a paradoxical state of both death and renewal, confusion
and opportunity, it is also a rite of passage and, therefore, predictable and manageable. One might say that the
initiate experiences a liminal state only within a culture
that remains foundational and centered. There are fixed
points of reference both before the experience and after.
Thus it is a normative experience with fairly predictable
results.

The Liminal and Religious Experience

Turner's account of liminality addresses these rites of passage as primary moments of religious experience. He suggests that religious experiences occur most intensely in these exceptional or transitional phases of life. These are times of heightened, exceptional, religious connection. The liminal individual may have visions or be led through powerful religious encounters by priest or elder. In modern culture it is still possible to discover echoes of such transitional religious events. Rites of passage such as birth, baptism, initiation into orders and secret societies, Bar Mitzvah, marriage, and death each illustrate the remains of older, intensely religious rites of passage. Involvement in such liminal settings still can elicit powerful religious experiences. Every pastor recognizes this phenomenon. The rites of passage are critical liminal experiences of intensified religious feelings. The margins, therefore, become the place most characterized by the sacred.[6] The noumenal comes very near. In biblical literature this is seen in the early stages of Israel's wandering in the wilderness, a liminal experience characterized by an intense sense of the sacred. The liminal provides opportunity for renewed and intensified relationship with God.

In discussion of the church's marginality, this aspect is often neglected. However, it is one of the most potentially powerful and redemptive elements in the current experience. Liminal experiences in Scripture often had this result. In both Hosea and Exodus the desert is the place where Israel enters her most profound reshaping experiences of God. There the potential for a new future is forged. In Psalm 137 Israel has been thrust into a liminal experience of captivity. Confusion and the sense of betwixt-and-between is present. Captivity is like entering a dark tunnel. It creates an ambiguity toward the sacred. How is it possible to sing the Lord's song in a strange land? On the one hand, it seems almost impossible to carry on with the ritual life because of liminality. The role and status sets of Jerusalem have been violently removed. The first impulse is to weep and yearn for the past when everything was well and the rituals made sense. But later, what will emerge is a fresh reconfiguration of the people's relationship to God and, therefore, to the surrounding culture.

The Potential for the New in the Liminal Experience

Liminality, as threshold experience, places a group in a place of confusion. The state of betwixt-and-between is like death and loss. The impulse is to find a road back to the old life. The potential for transformation and renewal is limited. In comparison with its former social state, the liminal group is in an unstructured state. Old rules no longer apply; they simply will not work. Because of this fact, liminality becomes a place of undefined potential. Something new can be discovered. Here is the reason the liminal phase is pivotal. For the church, experiencing its life as marginality, it is critical to understand that this is a passage with distinct phases, one of which is the potential

for transformation. This may be one of the most important aspects of liminality for the current discussion of
missionary congregations. The decisions that are made in
this phase shape the future of the group both internally,
in terms of self-identity, and externally, in terms of relationship with others in the surrounding setting. Again,
this is illustrated in God's conversations with Israel in
Hosea. When the prophet speaks of the people's return
to the desert, he is reminding them of their paradigmatic
place of liminality. It will be in the desert that they will
be wooed by God once more, transformed into the chil-
dren of God. The opportunity that liminality brings is
the possibility of rediscovering what it means to be the
people of God.

The contemporary church is in much the same state. It
is awakening to life at the margins and yearning for the
past detente. Reflection on where God may be leading
and shaping the church for a new future remains to be
done. The churches stand at the threshold of the liminal.
They have not yet embraced the potential for transformation. In a modern society, empty of the social meaning
given to liminal experiences, it is a question whether this
more positive stage will be achieved.

Two Types of Liminality in Modern Societies

How can the notion of liminality be applied in modern,
complex societies? In its present form, the rites of passage description of liminality explains ritual process in
traditional societies. What application does this have to

the marginal experience of marginality in North American churches? We may begin to answer this question by returning to Turner's own discussion. He identifies two types of liminal experience. The first type may be called institutionalized liminality. Rites of passage in pre-industrial societies fit this typology. The second type Turner describes as "spontaneously generated in a situation of radical structural change" (1974:248). This form addresses the current situation of the churches in modern societies like North America. Here, what had been fundamental social principles defining the relationship of the church in the culture lose their efficacy, "their capacity to operate as axioms of social behaviour, and new modes of social organization emerge, at first to transect, and, later, to replace traditional ones" (:ibid.). When the legitimacy of assumed cardinal social relations is called into question and negated, the symbol system that reinforced such relationships ceases to convince people. The group given status by those symbols moves into liminality.

Liminality is paradoxical. It places a group in great tension. Even in complex societies the impulses of groups in the liminal state move in two directions at the same time: turning backward to recover the lost identity and risking moving forward. Set in these terms, it is possible to locate the North American churches. Currently, much of the shaping conversation is that of return. Beneath schemes of renewal and strategies of growth lie these liminal impulses of return and recovery.

How, then, is this second form of liminality applied

to modern, complex societies? Turner (1977) states that in large-scale societies it is applied

> to societies in which, as Durkheim puts it, "the domain of religion," if not perhaps ritual, has "contracted," become a matter of individual choices rather than universal corporate ascription, and where, with religious pluralism, there is sometimes a veritable market of religious wares. In these societies, symbols once central to the mobilization of ritual action, have tended to migrate directly or in disguise, through the cultural division of labour, into other domains: esthetics, politics, law, popular culture, and the like (:36).

Turner's discussion has several important aspects. First, he argues that liminal experiences are still to be found in modern society but not in the same way as in pre-industrial society. One reason for this is the migration of symbols from the religious to other areas of life. Often the liminal is not recognized because it has shifted out from its primarily religious, sacred base. Second, this shift creates a new kind of liminal experience. The contraction of religion and the migration of symbolic meaning create parallel experiences of marginalization. This liminality is different from that of the loss of center. Symbol migration has created a decentered context for the churches that is a new form of liminality.

In an earlier work Turner (1974:285) further suggested that "history itself seems to have its discernable liminal periods, which share certain distinctive features,

between relatively stabilized configurations of social relations and cultural values. Ours may be one of them."
Here he touches upon one of the most critical characteristics of the liminal experience in modernity. Ours
is a period in history of such massive change that the
whole of modernity can be described as being in a liminal situation. What Turner describes is far more than
a predictable passage within a society. Rather, the en-
tire culture is in an unpredictable transition. It is not
just a particular group within the society that has lost
its former, established social locale. Practically everyone
is in this situation. In a period of large-scale historical
change liminality becomes the pervasive social experience. This second form of liminality is very different
from that of preindustrial societies. The language of center and margin no longer makes sense as an account of
what is actually happening. Other models of description
are required in order adequately to understand the current
social location.

One's perception of social location shapes one's response to changes in the larger social structures. The
church's understanding of its changed social location will
determine its praxis. What is making this understanding so complex are the multiple kinds of pressure points
intersecting the current experience of the church. The
pressure and complexity for the churches come from the
fact that there are actually two differing but intersecting
types of liminality present in modern cultures.

The first relates the long-term change in relationship between church and modern culture, as already

described, resulting in the effective end of Christendom. Most marginality arguments function out of this perception. Larry Rasmussen (1993:28) speaks of the "exceptional" place religion holds in modern culture, "noting that modern religion is exceptional in its relegation to the margins of ordinary existence."

In modernity the church's social role has been shifted into the realm of personal, private piety. But this has not been a particularly difficult marginal experience. The public-private detente worked quite well because, in the language of postmodern discourse, there remained, at least formally, a meta-narrative that was Christian in character. Modernity functioned on the moral and spiritual fragments of Christendom. For the majority of churches, this form of liminality was not felt as marginalization. Certainly, the fact of marginality has shaped the religious context of North America. But, for most of the period following World War II, the experience of the churches has not been that of marginality. Indeed it has only been quite recently that the churches have been open to the notion that it is no longer "our" world. Despite the fact that symbols of identity had contracted, losing their pervasive influence, churches have remained relatively at peace in their social location because of this sense that the Christian ethos was the pervasive social context. But this has changed in most parts of North America.

The second and more significant liminality is connected to the more fundamental transition from modernity to postmodernity. The assumption that this is "our culture" is quickly disintegrating. As a result there has emerged a growing concern about the marginal state of Christianity and, along with this, a renewal of the question of a missionary encounter with our culture. The two cannot be separated; the one follows from the other. This can be a hopeful sign if the church is able to conceive a genuinely post-Christendom ecclesiology. This second liminal form, then, relates to modernity's own fundamental transitions. Although these are pervasive, as yet they are not well-defined. The language used to describe these changes illustrates this. Zygmunt Bauman (1992:viii–ix) writes that "the postmodern state of mind is the radical ... victory of modern (that is, an inherently critical, restless, unsatisfied, insatiable) culture over the modern society it aimed to improve through throwing it wide open to its own potential" of a *universal dismantling of power-supported structures*" (emphasis in original), and the new postmodern mind's job as a "sort of site-clearing operation." In the famous words of Lyotard (1984:xxiv), "there now exists an incredulity toward meta-narratives." Although one may critique the imperialism of Lyotard's hyperbolic language, the overall tenor of his point is clear. A broad loss of belief in any overarching authority is the current reality. In contrast to preindustrial societies and much of modernity, there no longer exist norms that provide coherence and frameworks for the change processes through which we are moving. The culture is uncoupled from its foundational symbols. It is decentered from previous norms. Consequently, it is not marginalization that shapes our context but a liminality without center points

from which to gain perspective or meaning. What remains is a plethora of conflicting and competing symbols
and stories, each presented as interpretive of the current
liminal experience. No fixed points of reference remain
as normative. For most this has resulted in disorientation
and loss of confidence in a universe seemingly empty of
truth. This discontinuity is interpreted as marginalization; but that is an erroneous perspective, suited to the
earlier liminality of modernity and no longer useful in a
postmodern context.

It is in this double loop liminality that the churches
experience marginalization. The Christianity of modernity has been moving through this first loop for the past
several centuries. This has been a period of separation
when the symbols that once gave it place and identity
weakened and lost their power. This can be observed in
architecture (see Sennett 1990:10–19). Cathedrals and
churches in the premodern period functioned as places of
refuge and commerce as well as centers of worship. Their
architecture symbolized both God's immanence and transcendence through interior space. Vaulted ceilings drew
the eye upward to a destination beyond the roof. Cru-
ciform design symbolized the centrality of Christ in
the midst of the people. Interior architecture carried,
symbolically, the religious experience of the people. It
exemplified a society in harmony with its inner/outer,
public/private life. The world outside the church was not
separate from the world inside the building in the sense
that people understood intuitively where God could be
found. God's social location lay, architecturally, *inside* the

culture. At the same time, this *inside* was also the *center* of the culture. The cathedral was *the public* gathering place. Thus the architectural symbol of the cathedral represented the *inside-outside* and *center-periphery*, the *public center* of the culture. The church was both inside and at the center. The well-planned, regular, *inner* design of church or cathedral stood in symbolic contrast to the disorganized, irregular, *outer* construction of city houses and marketplaces. This contrast and sharp distinction gave to the religious symbol of the cathedral the power of being the cultural center. As Sennett (:16) points out, "making space sacred through definitions that contrasted to secular irregularity became a mark of Western urbanism."

All these symbolic relationships changed with the development of modernity. By the nineteenth century, the *inner-outer, center-periphery* dynamic of the medieval period had been radically displaced. This can be observed in the way another symbol was added to many of the older churches — the steeple. In the original construction of these buildings, height, with its attendant symbolism of transcendence, "was a matter of looking up from within, in the act of prayer, and so of having a visual experience of the Ascension." The steeples were "evidently added on the principle of emphasis: the more the better, in this case the higher the more spiritual" (:15). But there is also another kind of emphasis functioning in these nineteenth-century additions. It is important to note the spatial locale of this symbol in terms of *inside-outside, center-periphery* imagery. It was located on the *outside* of the building, constructed where the public world, outside the architectural symbols of religion, could see and identify the place where God was to be found. The shift is subtle but the message clear: as the two worlds separate, the steeple, an external symbol added to older architectural forms, becomes a means of connecting the new *inside*, the secular, with a new *outside*, the religious. The symbol of the church was no longer one that held together the inner/outer values of the culture. On the contrary, something had to be added to the architectural forms to help people locate the religious symbols in a changing society.

This first liminal loop, then, relates to the Christendom argument and the attendant declarations of its *effective* end. At the same time, using Turner's threefold account of liminality, one can make the case that what has actually happened, in relation to this first form of liminality, is that Christianity in the West has, to a large degree, moved through each of these phases. It has reintegrated itself back into the culture, albeit in a different social location and profoundly transformed. Signs of this are relatively easy to identify. The separation section has been illustrated and documented in numerous studies. The liminal phase of displacement was experienced as marginality. Former symbols of identity no longer kept Christianity at the center, and their power to hold people diminished. Throw up a thousand spires higher than the Sears Tower, but they no longer have the power to attract. Spend $100,000 repairing the organ, and still people will not come. This phase of liminality is the end point of separation; the group is outside the mainstream. Liminality is a betwixt-and-between experience. The tension is between discovering a means of getting back to the former social location or anticipating a transformational relationship with the society. For Christian churches in modernity, the primary pull was to define themselves in terms of what was deemed the center.

The church's acceptance of the public-private shift and its acceptance of relocation to the private world of inner, personal piety accounts for the way the liminal was negotiated in order to reenter the social context of modernity. The new center was a public world of the secular. Christianity accepted this arrangement and lived well within the detente modernity imposed upon the religious world. The Christian leadership was resymbolized in terms of professional, technician, and therapist. Such reshaping constituted the reintegration phase of the churches. The churches reintegrated with modernity in a new form. The end of Christendom was not experienced for very long as a marginal state. The churches inhabited their new private center exceptionally well. Indeed, many still do.

It is the second form of liminality that is at issue today, and this is not an issue of center-periphery but something quite different. In complex, modern cultures, this form of liminality still tends to result in an accentuated experience of the margins. But marginal notions are an inaccurate accounting. When the whole culture is in transformation, it is more than specific groups that find themselves in a changed social location. Different dynamics are at work.

Pastoral Identity and Liminality

Churches today must negotiate a path through this double liminality. The problem is that the first, with its resultant marginalization, masks the second, which is not an issue of marginalization. The result is complexity and confusion. Because liminality is a threshold experience — this paradoxical state of both death and renewal, confusion and opportunity — initially a group's psycho-social location makes it difficult to initiate the reflection required to think in terms of alternative frameworks. The experience of marginalization is too overpowering. In this situation the impetus is directed toward finding ways of quickly reintegrating with the culture.

One example of this process at work in the contemporary church is that of the pastor. Today pastors find themselves in the midst of complex changes where their traditional social roles have ceased to have the place and influence they once held. The symbol "pastor" has lost its power, and the function of priest has both constricted and migrated into other more "secular" religious forms. This is a liminal, betwixt-and-between time for pastors, their roles no longer fit the classifications of society. Questions are legitimately asked: What is a pastor? What do pastors do? Where do they fit? What kind of social function do they have? The further one moves into liminality, the greater the cognitive confusion about the designation of the role. This also creates greater pressure for pastor, denomination, and seminary to elicit forms of symbolic designation that will reintegrate the pastor into the center of social function. This is a ferment that now engages all these levels.

At this stage the temptation is to find a symbolic reintegration of pastoral identity and a role fit to deal with the loss of symbolic identity. But many of these roles are borrowed from symbols that have place and prominence in the wider culture. What this suggests is that the level of role confusion for the pastor in liminality is extremely high. For example, the pastor is clinician (therapeutic metaphor), chaplain (institutional metaphor), coach (sports metaphor), entrepreneur, marketer, and strategist (business metaphors). Besides the Bible, pastors must read John Bradshaw, know the Twelve Step process, discuss codependence, and memorize the business strategies of Attila the Hun and understand the new nonlateral leadership paradigm of Peter Senge. In a parallel manner, denominational judicatories reemphasize identity through credentials and certification. This stress on professional accreditation and the adding of new degrees after the pastor's name indicates the level of reintegration sought on the terms of the culture's own role values. The pastor is not only to be "professional" but must now become "Doctor," while the language of "Reverend" is cast overboard as a hangover from a previous age with a different perspective on role status. The point is that beneath all this casting about for appropriate symbolic nomenclature is a strained effort at recovery of role and identity. These new role terms are borrowed symbols of credibility and identity in a society that has declassified the pastoral identity. Much of this borrowing is an attempt to deny or bypass the experience of liminality rather than to recognize and embrace its reality. No wonder it is so difficult to be a pastor today!

The news, potentially, is not all bad. Liminality is also a place of opportunity, creativity, and transformation. In liminality we can recognize inappropriate metaphors and rediscover foundational symbols and images for the church and its leadership. The biblical tradition is full of such images waiting for reappropriation in the unsettling land of liminality. We need such a recovery. Technicians — mechanics of the latest method offering two hundred, sure-fire, guaranteed-to-work ways of making your congregation the most alive, fastest-growing, seeker-sensitive, liturgical, charismatic church in North America — are not qualified to chart the course ahead for the church. Nor is this new location a place for those wanting to be king of the castle. Turner makes an extremely insightful and important comment about hierarchies and status. If a group assumes that it resides at the center of a society, for example, as did the church and the papacy in the high Middle Ages, then it assumes all the trappings of power and authority embedded in that culture's self-understanding. Even though the pope was crowned and called upon to be *"servus servorum Dei,"* the reality was the inversion of this call. Hierarchies are controlled and shaped by the most powerful — those most "inside" the social center. This was not a problem in the Middle Ages. But today it is a major impediment to transformation. It remains with us in the

characterization of pastoral leadership in terms of entrepreneurial skills. Often it is difficult to tell whether the
pastor graduated from a seminary or a business school.
When a group enters the liminal phase, "the underling
becomes uppermost" (Turner 1969:102). This suggests
that the church will rediscover resources for a hopeful,
missionary-shaped future not only as it reengages the
Scripture, but also by listening to the voices of those
Christian groups that have long lived outside the center of our culture. It is in the dissenting churches and
what we have called the ethnic groups that our sources
of future direction will emerge. They understand the position of the underling and outsider. Liminality requires
us to listen attentively to their ecclesiologies. The biblical tradition emphasizes God's dealing with us from the
underside. It is from below that hope for new direction
emerges. This is why Jesus' coming was so confusing and
was resisted by the hierarchies of his time. The authen-
ticity of the gospel and the church is recovered by those
who, rather than being at the center, are functioning on
the periphery.

The church in modernity is in liminality. Rather than
seeing this as a great failure and loss, it is a work of the
Spirit inviting the church to rediscover its missional heart
in unimagined and unexpected places. One fears that in
North America, rather than hearing this call of the Spirit
to embrace and listen to the voice of God in a place of
strangeness, the churches are continuing to work hard at
rediscovering modes of existence and symbols of power
that will move them back to an imaginary center. A re-

turn to a remembered Christendom or the old detente with modernity is impossible. Those doors are closed. The only meaningful way forward lies in understanding and embracing our liminal existence. We must live with its confusion and humiliation, as a hopeful people ready to discover the new thing the Spirit will birth. The continued assumption of cultural symbols of power and success will only produce an inauthentic church with little gospel, much religion, and no mission. Liminality requires listening again to those voices emanating from below or outside the perceived mainstream.

The Liminal and the Liminoid

In describing the meaning of liminality for complex societies, Turner introduces the term *liminoid*. He differentiates between the liminal and the liminoid. In the liminal there is an overarching whole in which the various parts hang together. In the liminoid, that overarching meaning framework is absent; things have split apart into fragments and specializations with disparate directions and functions. Although Turner does not frame his comparison in these terms, the liminal can be identified with rites of passage in preindustrial cultures. The liminoid can be identified with complex modern cultures. In the former, the world is always returned to where it was before; things are righted so they make sense in an integrated whole. This describes the undercurrents in much of the re-forming and renewal in the churches. The need for a return to a stable, integrated order where place and identity are recognized and reintegrated in the social nexus remains high.

In the liminoid there is no returning to where the world was before, only movement into a future that continually undermines both the prevailing order and the nature of the sacred within the society. This double tension shapes the churches. On the one side remains the pull to return and overcome the loss of place; on the other, a culture where the center-periphery modalities are continually undermined by a constant flux of competing choices that configure and reconfigure in ever-differing forms.

The liminal is collective, connected to the calendric, biological, socio-structural cycles of a society. The liminoid is individualized, with little sense of cyclical or calenderized time. Significantly, the liminoid develops outside the central economic and political processes, along the margins. Potentially it is subversive of the larger society, representing radical critiques of central structures and offering alternative models for the future. Once more, this provides rich suggestions about where we need to be looking for hopeful missiologial directions.

In complex societies, the liminal represents not integration and passage but radical break and change. Because of this it has the power to call forth new, powerful symbols and forms that can radically transform both group and society. The opportunity of the liminoid is its power to subvert and transform from the outside with new models.

Communitas

Finally, Turner introduces into his discussion of liminality the term *communitas*. This is an important idea for churches addressing the question of a missionary encounter with modernity. Like any other group, churches are agents of socialization. They pass on meaning and identity in a double way. First, they communicate their own sociality, and second they communicate the values of the dominant culture. The churches have contributed powerfully to the second form of socialization. One of their main characteristics over the last half century has been this power to socialize members into the culture. Church and good citizenship have been synonymous. Positively, this contributes to the stabilization of society and, to this extent, is a good thing. What has been absent is the other, more important element of the church's calling, namely, the transformation of culture through its own sociality as an alternative community. In a liminal situation, it is this element that surely must be primary. A missionary encounter with modernity presupposes some form of transformational model for the church in relation to culture. The notion of communitas, as an essential element in liminality, offers this opportunity.

Because in both liminal and liminoid phases the group is removed from prior sets of symbols and relationships, normal networks of classification and position in the cultural space no longer hold. In the liminoid, prior normative ranks and hierarchies of relationship and status lose their power to determine and shape the group. Egalitarianism and comradeship come to the fore. People discover one another on a level different from that experienced when the group viewed itself as a structured, nonliminal part of the larger culture. What is possible is the recognition, or recovered awareness, however fleeting, of a social bond that has ceased to be — in other words, the possibility of rediscovering the essential tradition foundational for the group, the essence of what it means to be God's people.

Behind the perspective of communitas lie two alternative models of human relationship. Turner describes these in terms of "structure" and "communitas." Structure refers to the normative understanding of a society as a structured, differentiated, hierarchical system of politico-legal-economic positions. Robert Merton (in Turner 1977:46) describes this as "the patterned arrangements of role-sets, status-sets, and status-sequences" on the whole consciously recognized and regularly operative in a given society. When we participate in social structure, thus regarded, we are presented with an orderly social world, a recognized system of social control, prescribed ways of acting toward people by virtue of our incumbency of status-roles. In a "structure" context immediacy tends to be lost, people are constrained by laws and conventions, and they are usually limited in the degree to which they can "play" with ideas or innovate behavior.

Several aspects of this description are important. First, it describes the "Christendom" modality of the churches that has ceased to exist. It also aptly sketches how denominations and congregations continue to understand their function. They operate out of status roles based upon an assumed place within the larger social structure. One way in which this is evident is the reformulation of congregational life following World War II as the majority of churches switched to the new suburbs. A study of the organizational shape of these congregations and the reshaping of denominational judicatories indicates a pattern of organizational forms parallel to the new corporate structures in which most suburban churchgoers worked. This reshaping along the lines of the structural functions of the society suggests the church's comfort with its place at the heart of the culture, even if that heart was the private world.

But what is impossible in this situation is what Turner calls "play." There is little room to dream, to think outside the lines of modernity, or to envision an alternative future. This is seen through a study of the many "alternative" models and accounts of how to be the church that emerged following World War II, another liminal period in the life of North America that brought with it a great deal of creativity in envisioning the future of congregational life. Despite the number of studies and books written, all of that creativity and vision resulted in very little permanent change in congregational life or in mission beyond a new aggregation within the suburbs. Little would change in the ensuing decades (Winter 1961).

Part of the ferment within churches today stems from the fact that their postwar status roles have eroded. The question of a missionary encounter with modernity indicates that there is a growing recognition of liminality among the churches. They are searching for a location in the new social context. Positively, as at the midpoint of this century, the potential to dream and envision is present. The rediscovery of social bonds rooted in the gospel is again possible. The tension is that, as in the postwar period, the churches will once more look for status roles in the culture and so define their life by norms within the society. It would be a great tragedy to allow this present moment of opportunity to pass without effecting fundamental transformation.

The second, contrasting form of human relatedness is what Turner calls communitas. In the liminoid state the group's life has become unglued and unstructured in relation to its former place. This promises to produce the optimal conditions for the emergence of communitas. The stripping of former roles and status "may have the effect of strengthening the bonds of communitas even as it dissolves antecedent social structural ties" (Turner 1969:47). Communitas suggests the formation of a new peoplehood, the constitution of a new vision for being a group. The basis of recruitment is no longer status or role function but identity and belonging within a group that, in some clear ways, stands outside the mainstream of the culture. Although Turner recognizes that communitas can devolve into unhealthy subgroups, as in totalitarian sects or the communities of self-interest reported by Bellah (1985), it becomes crucial "to keep the pipeline open between the society in general and each of its communitas groups" (Turner 1977:47) in order to

Trying to marginalize the church

avoid a narrow sectarianism that insulates and removes the group from the culture, creating yet another type of apolitical church.

Negatively, communitas, as with liminality in general, can become a means of spiritualizing the church's existence in terms of a sectarian community whose identity and future lie outside this world. This is a potential response when the experience of marginality intensifies the group's own sense of identity over against the larger culture. The reemergence of highly affective, experience-oriented groups shaped by nonrational accounts of God's presence constitutes the presence of this possibility. Emphasis upon certain kinds of signs and wonders as experiential guarantees of the group's relatedness to God in a hostile world is a harbinger of this more spiritualized type of communitas. Clearly, there are dangers to be guarded against. Not only is there pressure to reintegrate with the culture on its terms but also to form decontextualized communities claiming special revelations of God's activity in the world. These kinds of communitas tend to see themselves as the church within the church.

How do the churches create a communitas that responds to the deep malaise and contemporary experience of people in North America? What is required is a communitas that calls forth an alternative vision for the social and political issues facing the people. A fitting image for this communitas is the city on a hill that Jesus used to anticipate the new social reality he was calling into being. This is a distinct but visible society offering an alternative form of life. This is the way Christianity entered history. It was a new social reality formed out of a liminal experience that created the communitas of a new peoplehood. It took the form of a group existing on the edges of the social worlds of its time. It was a distinct and peculiar people with a strong sense of belonging to one another. The social status of hierarchy and power, embedded in the structures of the larger culture, were radically questioned, as one notes in the early experience of women in the church. For Paul, the gospel relativized and transcended status based on race, gender, social rank, and culture in a new peoplehood under Christ. New Testament writers took older symbols and images, such as royal priesthood, chosen people, and holy nation, and transformed them in order to give form and meaning to this new reality of the church. The early church resisted the temptation to subsume itself beneath the larger categories of its social setting but did identify and relate to the fundamental malaise of the people in that period (Dodds 1965:chap. 12). The churches were shaped by a different reality and so, in the end, transformed their culture.

A similar potential resides in our current liminal experience in a pluralized culture. But the danger of merely accommodating to the categories of our time and place in North America is immense. The captivity of the church is so deep and pervasive, the church's own symbols so fundamentally co-opted, that at present it is difficult to imagine how these symbols can engage our culture in a way similar to the early church. The question for any missional ecclesiology is how to call forth this new community. This is the most difficult issue now facing us, but some directions for a way ahead can be outlined.

The promise of communitas is the potential of rediscovering the tradition as a reservoir for transformation. Communitas offers an alternative to the central perversion of the church in modernity, its individualized and privatized spirituality, which, as an inheritance from the Romantic movement, represents an accommodation of the person to modernity. This leaves not so much self-centered individuals as diminished, shadow people, vulnerable to the shaping and forming of modernity. Communitas offers the reconversion of the church for its missionary encounter with modern culture. Indeed, only this form of life can possibly provide the means for an engagement with our culture that will remain faithful to the biblical witness. This is the primary opportunity liminality offers: the church in modernity can recover its communal sense of being God's people. It is this notion of communitas that suggests how the church may create its own determinate social world, the city on a hill. In this social reality, the core of identity has shifted from institutional to communal relationships. Instead of status, place, and law, there is the intersubjectivity of persons formed by a new center, Jesus Christ as the head of the communitas.

What is suggestive here is that in modernity the epistemological center of faith is no longer the privatized individual's inner piety but the community. Personal identity is shaped through membership in the communitas. This will be a difficult journey. Liminality requires a missionary ecclesiology that cannot return to the pre-industrial world to create some decontextualized community, nor can it simply become a constructed artifact of modernity, a technique learned at some workshop. The difficult task is to define the meaning of communitas in our culture. In one sense there is nothing new in what is being proposed. But it remains to be given reality in our setting. What follows represents suggestions for that movement in terms of the primary leadership of congregations. Pastors are the ones who bear the greatest role in the shaping of missionary congregations.

3

Toward a Missionary Ecclesiology

___

graduates?

Liminality requires leaders with the theological, political, and social skills to elicit the new communitas. This involves not just technique but the art of memory and expectation in which the lived experience of the past is indwelt in order for it to become our experience once more. This requires leaders whose identity is formed by the tradition rather than the culture. It also requires leaders who listen to the voices from the edge. This is where the apostle, the prophet, and the poet are found. These are the metaphors for congregational leadership today. The pastor's ears must be attuned not primarily to the popular, the latest trend, or the expert, but to those who recognize that marginality is the church's reality. By the waters of Babylon there is no way back to the old Jerusalem. Liminality requires a different kind of leader if congregations are to be encountered by and encounter our culture with the gospel.

Pastor/Poet

The pastoral function must be reinterpreted in light of this need to create a communitas as the fundamental missionary nature of the congregation. The pastoral role in the context of liminality is that of articulating the congregation's experience in modernity. In this sense, pastors must reinterpret their roles not primarily as caregivers but as poets. Poets are the articulators of experience and the rememberers of tradition. They image and symbolize the unarticulated experiences of the community, identifying and expressing the soul of the people. The poet is a listener and an observer, sensing the experience of the body and giving that experience a voice. As poet, the pastor needs all the skills of pastoral care, but these skills are the servant of a larger end rather than ends in themselves.

Many voices speak in the church today at a superficial level. They speak of how our personal needs may be met, or of patching up the old ship so that it sails as it did before in the sea of culture, or of one more new method of renewal or evangelism. But the poet hears voices at a deeper level. The poet listens to the pain and questioning emerging from the fragmentation and alienation dwelling within modern people — the loneliness of our individualism as experienced by those in our congregations. The poet knows that these are cries for something more than self-development or techniques of success; they are cries that long to be connected to a Word that calls them beyond themselves into a place of belonging that God gives within a people. The poet's vocation is to bring these voices to expression so that we may listen again to the voice of God speaking into our situation of marginality. There will be no vision of a missionary people without the poet/pastor living within the congregation's experience and giving voice to its desire for transformation and renewal.

The pastor/poet does not begin by teaching ideas so that the congregation understands modernity. Rational accounting is not the first step. Paradigmatic change begins with reflection by the people of God on their own immersion in modernity. This, too, is an important part of discipleship. In such discourse the poet/pastor brings to voice their story so that there occurs a "Yes! This is who we are! This is who we meet when we touch the fear and confusion about being God's people in this culture!" The pastor weaves together the people's voices so that the story of who they are and what they actually experience is articulated, called forth, and owned. In this process the tapestry of their lives is made visible. This is, in part, what Scripture means about speaking the truth in love. As we are brought to the truth about ourselves, we are opened to hear the gospel anew. Such poetry writing begins the process of calling out an alternative vision for God's people. But pastors cannot be such poets unless they reflect upon their own experiences as persons of faith in modernity. This, in turn, requires intellectual reflection on the meaning and contours of this land in which the gospel lives as a stranger. The poet is of no pastoral use to the congregation if all she or he can do is express feelings of personal anxiety and confusion.

Such poetry is little more than therapy, the reconditioning of people to live in the ambiguity of their context. Rather, the poet writes so that the congregation hears their story as God's pilgrim people. This means writing with as much intellectual engagement with the culture as passion for the experience of the people. The tapestry must be woven of both elements before the possibility of transformation can emerge in the condition of liminality.

Pastor/Prophet

It is clear from the description of liminality that one of the most important roles of congregational leadership in this time is to recover the prophetic. Prophecy is the addressing of the Word of God directly into the specific, concrete historical experience of the people of God. Unless the gospel addresses God's people we are lost. The prophetic imagination directs the poetic discourse of the people toward a vision of God's purposes for them in the world at this time. The recognition, elicited through the poetic role, of the congregation that "we are this people living at the edges of modernity" finds hope for transformation as the biblical witness is brought to bear upon the community's experience. Without this other Word, the community turns its pain into the ghetto experience of marginalization rather than the recognition that it exists for the life of the world. Without the prophetic, poetic leadership is little more than adaptation and consolation. The prophet addresses the hard side of discipleship where we must face the reality that in God's kingdom we are not at the center of the universe.

In liminality, what is needed is the Word from the outside that gives a new vision and fresh definition to being God's people. Here the prophet engenders hope out of which arises authentic missional engagement. The prophetic word cuts across the assumption that we have been called to create the kingdom of God out of the kingdoms of this world. It re-presents the cosmic picture of Christ who came into the world to address the ideologies and structures that leave us dehumanized, as commodities to be manipulated, or as isolated individuals called to salvation by self-fulfillment. And this includes the ideologies within the churches that foster the belief that congregational life and practice are to be shaped by the exigencies of the popular. Here the pastor-as-prophet calls forth a different story of God's people, a people who are out on a missionary journey that calls them far beyond themselves, to a gospel that does not belong to any social order or ideology. The alternative community is not formed primarily through small-group ministries or seminars on how to be community for one another; it is formed as the prophetic word addresses the pained recognition of our liminality.

Pastor/Apostle

In liminality, pastors must lead congregations as witnesses to the gospel in lands where old maps no longer work. This requires an apostolic role. Hans Küng and others have rightly argued that the congregation is foundationally apostolic. But does it actually assume this role, given its captivity to modernity? In response, it is frequently suggested that congregations will become apostolic when pastors become equippers and disciplers. Ephesians 4:11–12 is used as the axiomatic text. This is fair enough, but it begs the question of how pastors equip and disciple? In a time when congregations are confused, ghettoized, and have few, if any, models of what it means to be a missionary people, how do pastors equip and disciple? Equipping and discipling must be more than small-group Bible studies on the gospel and culture. This is not to demean the place of Scripture, but we are a culture that believes that if something has been studied, then it has been done. Discipling and equipping require a leadership that demonstrates encounter with the culture in action. This is the role of the pastor as apostle. In the days ahead, the gown of the scholar must be replaced with the shoes of the apostle. This is not to diminish the importance of intellectual engagement, but is a call for a shift of paradigm toward contextual engagement with the culture. Pastor, as apostle, is foundational to all other functions.

In a broad sense of the term, the apostle is commissioned by Christ for missionary proclamation and strategy in the world. This is not just a matter of taking the gospel *into* the world and modeling for the congregation how to recruit members for the church. Rather, the apostle holds up the gospel in order that it may encounter the cultural context and challenge the congregation's need to be shaped by its calling to be apostolic. This approach stands in contradistinction to our instinctual images of pastor. For example, a pastor recently stated: "Pastoral care is the business we're in; if we're not preparing worship, we are doing pastoral care." Pastors are supposed to be *in the church* rather than *in the world*. In a Christendom model, this was the case. But such separations are not acceptable in a missionary situation. If we heed Lesslie Newbigin's call for missionary leaders, then the apostolic function must come to the fore.

Discussions of pastoral leadership center on roles *within* the congregation. Models are offered that shift leadership images from hierarchical to servant, from the top down to the bottom up. The image often used is that of a triangle. Rather than a triangle with a wide base, as in the accompanying diagram (p. 65), with the leader at the top and the people at the base of a hierarchy, renewalists call for an inverted triangle with the laity at the top and the pastor at the bottom, as servant. Redefining pastoral leadership in terms of servanthood and lay-empowerment is laudable, but the model is problematic. It swings the pendulum from one extreme to another, continuing the dichotomy between servant and directive leadership. They are not opposites. But of more critical importance, the servant/equipping model only rearranges the Christendom image of congregational leader as one whose role function is entirely *within* the church for the well-being of the people. Here pastor is a symbol of the ecclesiocentric nature of the church. This must change. The image of apostle is a powerful one for our day precisely because it is related so closely to a kingdom understanding rather than a church understanding of God's action in Christ. Further, the apostle is commissioned by Christ, and we need such strong images of leadership in order to move away from the current views of pastors as enculturated professionals hired by congregations to provide religious services.

Let us place the triangle on its side as an elongated wedge with a directional point. This diagram shows a church called to function as a mission band, directed toward the world and moving toward a destination other than its own self-preservation or inner growth.

The place of leadership is neither at the top nor the bottom; rather, it is at the leading edge of the triangle, modeling engagement with the culture in the name of the gospel. This is what is intended by the notion of apostolic leadership as primary and foundational for pastors today. Such a model shifts the pastoral role outward to the forefront of missional engagement.

This change entails structural implications. Pastor/apostle leadership cannot function in a *sola pastora* model. Rather than the omnicompetent professional running the congregation's inner life, there is a team, or multiple leadership, at the heart of the congregation. This does not imply professional staff. Indeed, it should not. Pastoral care, worship, proclamation, and administration are part of the work of the whole people of God, not the designated territory of someone with a seminary degree and an ordination certificate. The guild of the ordained will

Models of Structure

TRADITIONALIST

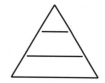

Pastor (Minister)

Leaders (Assistants)

Congregation

RENEWALIST

Congregation (Minister)

Leaders

Staff

Pastor

MISSIONAL

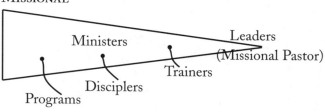

have to be removed; this is one social function that will not move us through liminality.

The pastor/apostle is one who forms congregations into mission groups shaped by encounters with the gospel in the culture — structuring the congregation's shape into forms that lead people outward into a missionary encounter. Discipleship emerges out of prayer, study, dialogue, and worship by a community learning to ask the questions of obedience *as they are engaged directly in mission*. But in this kind of congregation, the pastor will be able to lead only as she or he models the encounter with the culture.

Conclusion

In the introduction to his book *Earthing the Gospel,* Gerald Arbuckle writes about the confusion of the "sense of pastoral chaos the churches feel when confronted with a world in rapid cultural change." He argues that the chaos is so great today that the old ways do not work, and we can no longer speak in terms of renewal of the church but its re-founding. He says: "If re-founding is to occur, however, the church desperately needs people of imagination and creativity" (1990:2). This is the challenge facing churches that recognize the call for a missionary engagement with modernity.

Notes

1. This is not a new question in our century. Prior to and immediately following World War II, the World Council of Churches initiated and funded major projects focused on the missionary nature of the congregation. At the midcentury point, the churches addressed issues of secularization and a postcolonial world. These fruitful and important discussions failed to enter the mainstream of reflection about the nature of the church in North America. The reasons for this would be an important study for our own current situation but are not the locus of this conversation. One of the influential participants in those World Council proceedings was Lesslie Newbigin. His more recent writings have provided a framework for the current discussion in North America (Newbigin 1986 and 1989). In both the United Kingdom and North America, the development of Gospel and Our Culture Networks further indicates the growing significance of these questions.

2. This can be seen from a variety of writers as they diagnose the situation of the church in modernity. See, for example, David Wells (1993) and Stanley Hauerwas and William Willimon (1990). These represent divergent accounts of the problematic, but each functions out of the assumption that there has been a radical decentering of Christianity in modernity.

3. This approach can be seen in Reginald Bibby's book (1993). The first half of the book is basic sociological research on the attitudes of Canadians toward God, belief, and the churches. It is extremely helpful material. In the third section of the book, Bibby shifts from description and analysis to prescription. The underlying theme of that section is the market niche.

4. The phrase is from Ulf Hannerz (1992). Parts of the discussion in the following paragraphs use Hannerz's perspective.

5. see Philip Rieff (1987).

6. This might provide insight into current manifestations of intense experiences of the sacred among some charismatic groups. Such groups tend to be comprised of middle-class, educated adults in search of some connection with the sacred. For example, in places like the Toronto Airport Vineyard, which has been given major media coverage in *Time* magazine and the *Times* of London, shaking, barking, laughing, falling over, and convulsing the body are normative experiences. They are interpreted as primarily signs of God preparing and blessing God's people for a new revival. These signs are preparation for the revival. Thus they become liminal events that are preparing God's people for a new reintegration with the culture. The church is about to be revived; in its remade form it will function again in a Pentecost lifestyle. The manifestations become liminal experiences bringing with them a guarantee of an intense sense of the sacred. Current attraction to these kinds of experience may be more an indication of the anxiety that has overcome middle-class Christians because of the marginalization of Christianity than an actual sign of God's presence. This is not to deny that God is present in these contexts revealing love and care. People are attracted to these liminal events precisely because they seem to guarantee some form of connection with the sacred.

References Cited

Anderson, Ray. 1993. *Ministry on the Firing Line.* Downers Grove, Ill.: InterVarsity Press.

Arbuckle, Gerald. 1990. *Earthing the Gospel.* Maryknoll: Orbis Books.

Bauman, Zygmunt. 1992. *Intimations of Modernity.* New York: Routledge & Kegan Paul.

Bellah, Robert, et al. 1985. *Habits of the Heart: Individualism and Commitment in American Life.* Berkeley: University of California Press.

Bibby, Reginald W. 1993. *Unknown Gods: The Ongoing Story of Religion in Canada.* Toronto: Stoddart.

Conn, Harvie M. 1984. *Eternal Word and Changing Worlds: Theology, Anthropology, and Missions in Trialogue.* Grand Rapids: Zondervan Academic Books.

Dodds, E. R. 1965. *Pagan and Christian in an Age of Anxiety.* New York: W. W. Norton.

Gunton, Colin. 1993. *The One, The Three and the Many: God, Creation and the Culture of Modernity.* Cambridge: Cambridge University Press.

Hall, Douglas John. 1989. *Thinking the Faith: Christian Theology in a North American Context.* Minneapolis: Fortress Press.

————. 1993. Responses to the Humiliation of the Church. University of the South, School of Theology, Sewanee, Tennessee. *Sewanee Theological Review* 36, no. 4 (1993):472–81; Michaelmas, 1993.

Hannerz, Ulf. 1992. *Cultural Complexity: Studies in the Social Organization of Meaning.* New York: Columbia University Press.

Hauerwas, Stanley, and William H. Willimon. 1990. *Resident Aliens.* Nashville: Abingdon Press.